OUR CHANGING PLANET

Shrinking Wetlands

Kari Jones

Explore other books at:
WWW.ENGAGEBOOKS.COM

VANCOUVER, B.C.

WWW.ENGAGEBOOKS.COM

Shrinking Wetlands - Our Changing Planet: *Level 3*
Jones, Kari 1966 –
Text © 2023 Engage Books
Design © 2023 Engage Books

Edited by: A.R. Roumanis, Ashley Lee,
Melody Sun & Sarah Harvey
Design by: Mandy Christiansen

Text set in Montserrat Regular.
Chapter headings set in Animated Gothic Light.

FIRST EDITION / FIRST PRINTING

LIBRARY AND ARCHIVES CANADA CATALOGUING IN PUBLICATION

Title: Shrinking wetlands / Kari Jones.
Names: Jones, Kari (Kari Lynne), 1966- author.
Description: Series statement: Our changing planet

Identifiers: Canadiana (print) 2023044783X | Canadiana (ebook) 20230447848
ISBN 978-1-77476-899-0 (hardcover)
ISBN 978-1-77476-900-3 (softcover)
ISBN 978-1-77476-901-0 (epub)
ISBN 978-1-77476-902-7 (pdf)
ISBN 978-1-77878-126-1 (audio)

Subjects:
LCSH: Wetlands—Juvenile literature.
LCSH: Wetland conservation—Juvenile literature.
LCSH: Nature—Effect of human beings on—Juvenile literature.

Classification: LCC QH541.5.M3 J66 2023 | DDC J577.68—DC23

This project has been made possible in part
by the Government of Canada.

Canada

Contents

What Are Wetlands?

Wetlands are areas of land that are covered by water. Some wetlands are only covered in water for part of the year. Others are covered year-round. They are important **ecosystems**.

KEY WORD

Ecosystems: communities of living and nonliving things that work together to stay healthy.

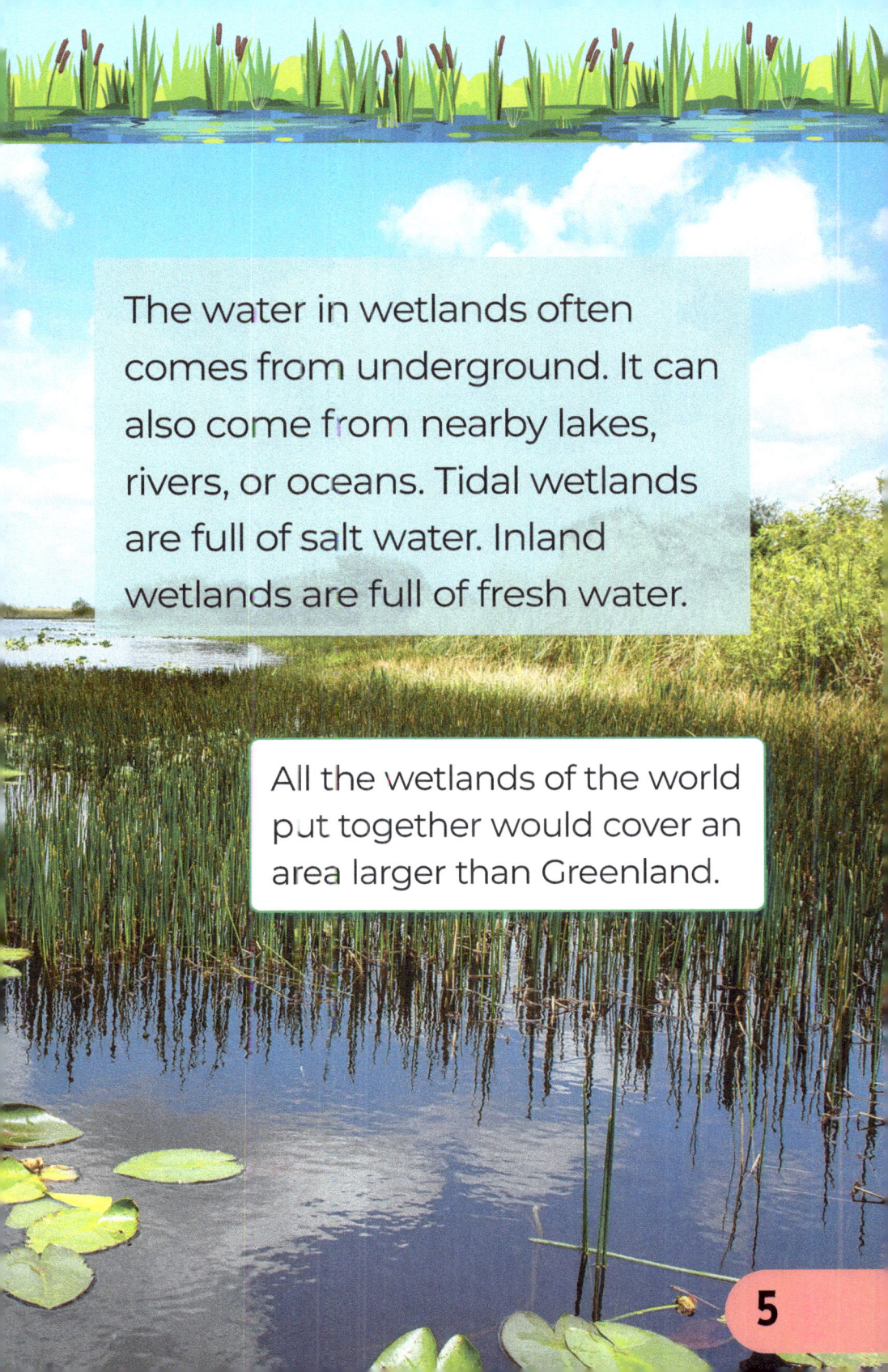

The water in wetlands often comes from underground. It can also come from nearby lakes, rivers, or oceans. Tidal wetlands are full of salt water. Inland wetlands are full of fresh water.

All the wetlands of the world put together would cover an area larger than Greenland.

A Closer Look

There are many different kinds of wetlands all around the world. The only place wetlands are not found is in Antarctica. Some of the most common wetlands are marshes, swamps, and bogs.

Different wetlands have different **species** of plants and animals. Plants with soft stems are common in marshes. Swamps have lots of trees like mangroves. Bogs are often covered in a plant called moss.

Species: a group of similar animals or plants that can make babies with each other.

What Does It Mean if a Wetland Is Shrinking?

If a wetland is shrinking, that means it is getting smaller. It is becoming dry. If it gets too small, it will disappear.

About 35 percent of the world's wetlands disappeared between 1970 and 2015.

Wetlands are one of the fastest disappearing ecosystems in the world. They are disappearing three times faster than the world's forests. The United States could lose 75 percent of its **coastal** wetlands by 2100.

KEY WORD

Coastal: close to where the land meets the ocean.

Why Are Wetlands Shrinking 1?

People sometimes build **dams** on rivers or streams. They do this to collect water for people in cities. This water can no longer reach wetlands. This causes them to dry out.

KEY WORD

Dams: large walls that stop water from flowing.

Many wetlands are shrinking as people build larger farms. Water is taken out of wetlands so the land can be used to grow food or raise animals. Over one-third of the world's land is used for **agriculture**.

11

Why Are Wetlands Shrinking 2?

Invasive species of plants and animals take over wetlands. They kill the species that used to live there. Invasive mussels have destroyed wetlands across North America.

TEXAS PARKS & WILDLIFE

ADVISORY

ZEBRA MUSSELS
ARE IN THIS WATER BODY

CLEAN your boat, trailer and gear. Remove all plants, mud and debris before leaving the ramp.

DRAIN all water from boat, motor, bait buckets and any compartments.

DRY a week or more, or power wash everything with hot, soapy water before visiting another water body.

PROTECT THE LAKES YOU LOVE. STOP INVASIVE SPECIES.
Zebra mussels attached to your boat? Call TPWD before moving it! (512) 389-4848
TPWD.TEXAS.GOV/ZEBRAMUSSELS

KEY WORD

Invasive species: a plant or animal that does not naturally live in an area.

Earth's temperature is rising because of **climate change**. Warmer weather causes more fires and long periods of time without rain. These events can damage wetlands or cause them to dry out.

KEY WORD

Climate change: a change in the average temperature over a long period of time.

Effects on the Planet

Wetlands store **carbon**. This helps keep the planet's temperature down. Carbon is released into the air when wetlands dry out.

> **KEY WORD**
>
> **Carbon:** a gas that adds to climate change by causing Earth to get warmer.

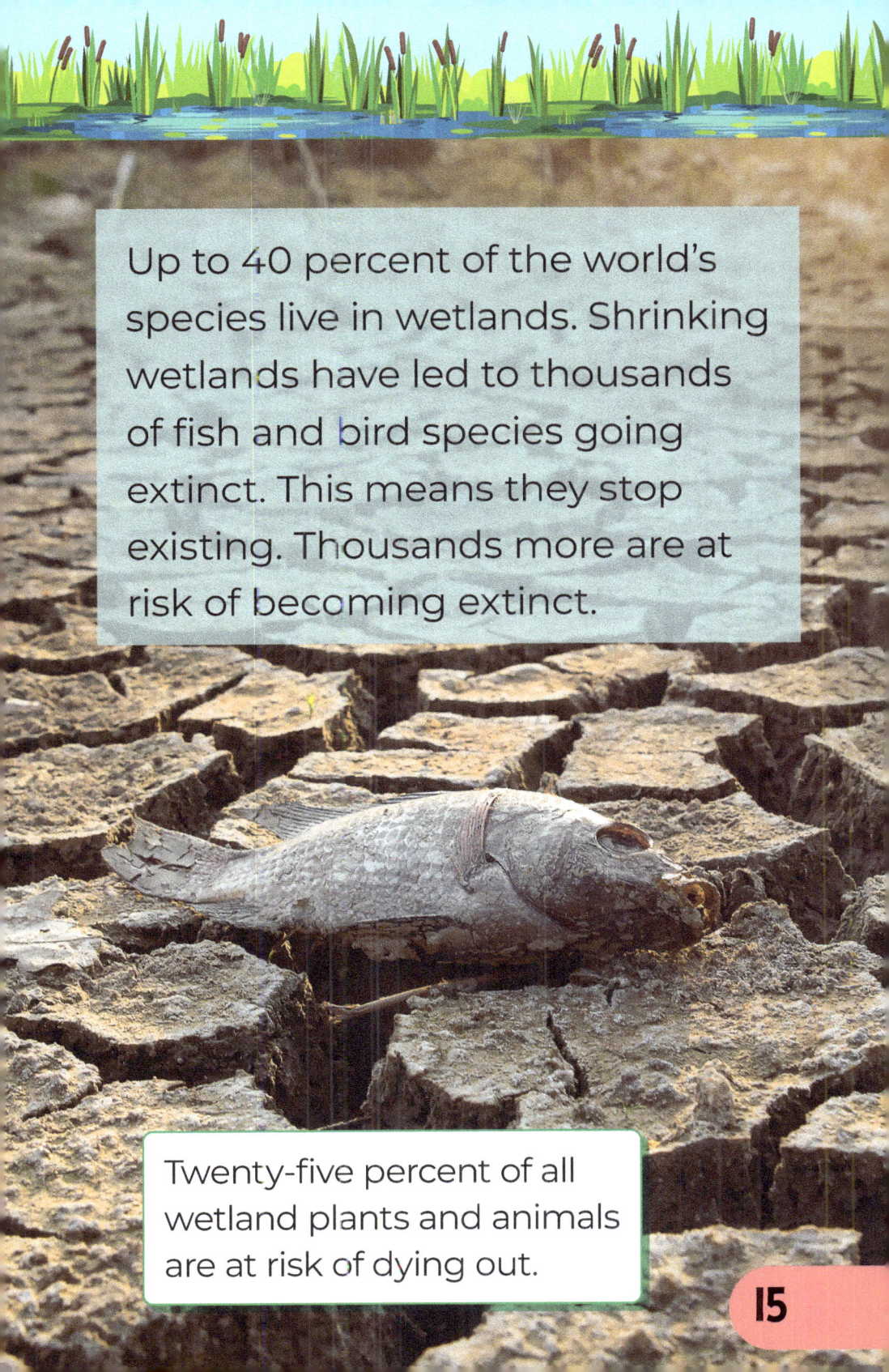

Up to 40 percent of the world's species live in wetlands. Shrinking wetlands have led to thousands of fish and bird species going extinct. This means they stop existing. Thousands more are at risk of becoming extinct.

Twenty-five percent of all wetland plants and animals are at risk of dying out.

Effects on Humans

Wetlands are able to stop small amounts of dirt and chemicals from reaching other bodies of water. This helps keep water clean. Many people drink this water and eat the plants and animals found in wetlands. Shrinking wetlands means less clean drinking water and less food for people.

Some wetlands are the only source of food and water for people living nearby. Shrinking wetlands are causing these people to leave their homes. They have to find other sources of food and water.

Wetlands provide food and water for more than one billion people.

Wetlands Around the World 1

Thirty percent of the plants and animals in the **Mediterranean Basin** need wetlands to live. This area lost about half of its wetlands during the 1900s. This was mostly because of growing farms and cities.

KEY WORD

Mediterranean Basin: the lands around the Mediterranean Sea.

Many people live in houseboats near the Vembanad-Kol wetlands in India. These wetlands have been shrinking because of growing towns. The water has also been **polluted** by garbage and chemicals.

Wetlands Around the World 2

The Mekong Delta wetlands help feed millions of people in Vietnam and Cambodia. Parts of these wetlands are drying out. Other areas are being polluted with waste.

The Pantanal in South America is the world's largest **tropical** wetland. Parts of the Pantanal are protected by the government. Most of it is in danger of being taken over by farms.

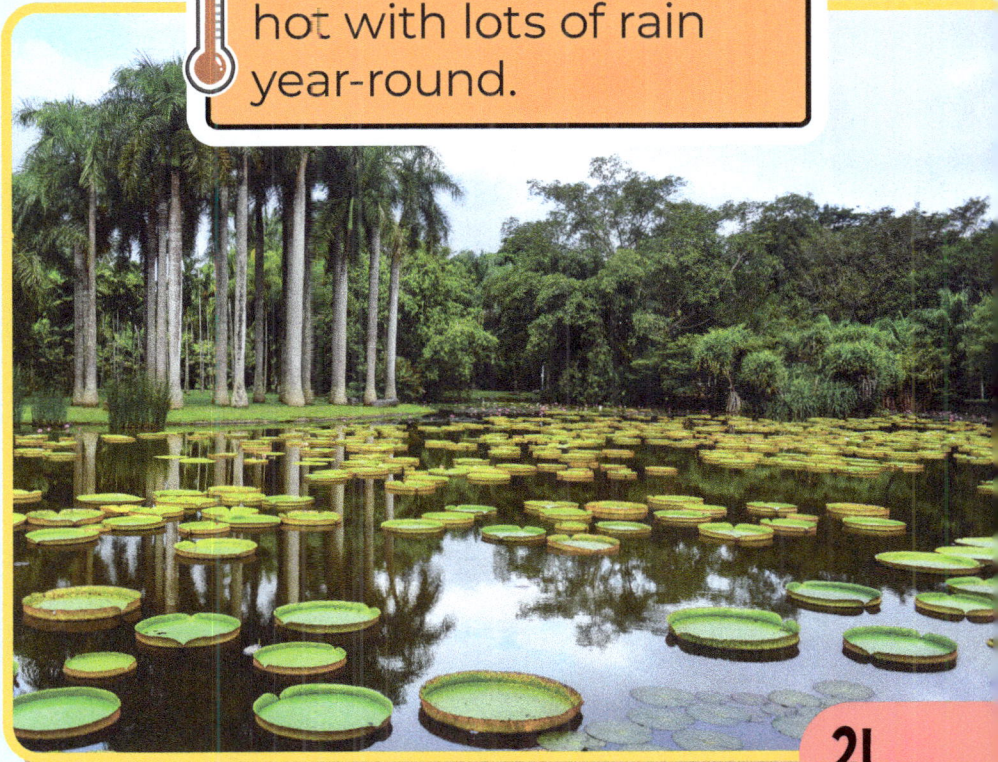

Shrinking Wetlands Solutions 1

The Ramsar Convention on Wetlands is a group of more than 170 countries. They are protecting wetlands around the world. These countries make laws that do not allow certain wetlands to be destroyed.

The Ramsar Convention started World Wetlands Day. Governments and schools have events to teach people about the importance of wetlands. This helps people learn how to take care of the wetlands in their area.

World Wetlands Day takes place on February 2.

WORLD WETLANDS DAY
FEBRUARY 2

Shrinking Wetlands Solutions 2

Citizen scientists are watching wetlands and writing down what they see. They look at the plants and animals found there and how much water there is. They send this information to scientists.

KEY WORD

Citizen scientists: people who are not scientists who collect information and send it to scientists.

Scientists cannot look at all the wetlands in the world. Citizen scientists help collect more information than scientists would be able to collect on their own. Scientists can use this information to figure out what each wetland needs to stay healthy.

The Helpers

A group called Youth Engaged in Wetlands works to protect wetlands and keep them healthy. It is made up of young people from all around the world. They sometimes go to Ramsar Convention meetings and work with them.

Wetlands International has been protecting wetlands since 1937. They have **offices** in 20 different countries to help wetlands all around the world. Their work helps local communities that need wetlands for food and water.

How Can You Help?

If you live near a wetland, help remove invasive plants from the area. Cleanup groups are often looking for help with this. Ask a local **naturalist** how you can do this without harming the animals or other plants that live there.

KEY WORD

Naturalist: someone who studies animals and plants.

If you travel to a wetland, stay in the areas meant for visitors. If you have a dog, keep them on a leash when you go for walks. They could damage the wetland if they run through it. They could also harm any animals that live there.

Quiz

Test your knowledge of shrinking wetlands by answering the following questions. The questions are based on what you have read in this book. The answers are listed on the bottom of the next page.

1 What are wetlands?

2 What does it mean if a wetland is shrinking?

3 What is released into the air when wetlands dry out?

4 How many people do wetlands provide food and water for?

5 What is the world's largest tropical wetland?

6 When is World Wetlands Day?

Explore Other Level 3 Readers.

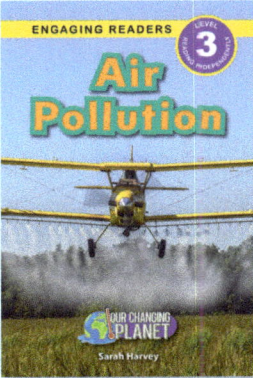

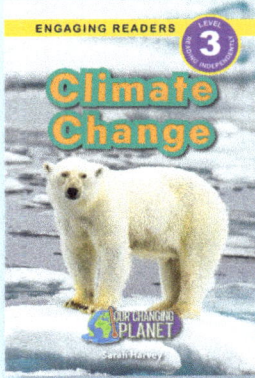

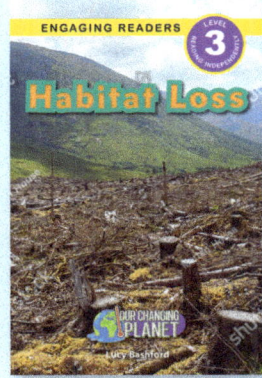

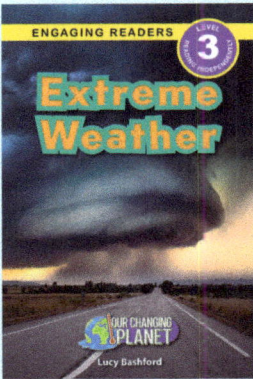

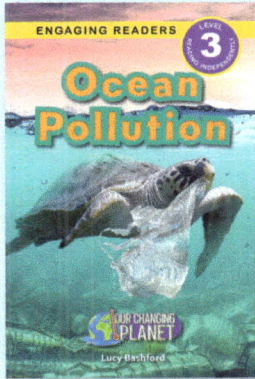

ENGAGING READERS — LEVEL 3

Air Pollution
OUR CHANGING PLANET
Sarah Harvey

Climate Change
OUR CHANGING PLANET
Sarah Harvey

Habitat Loss
OUR CHANGING PLANET
Lucy Bashford

Extreme Weather
OUR CHANGING PLANET
Lucy Bashford

Ocean Pollution
OUR CHANGING PLANET
Lucy Bashford

Diabetes
Mind and Body
Kit Caudron-Robinson

Obesity
Mind and Body
Kit Caudron-Robinson

Autism
Mind and Body
AJ Knight

Vision Loss
Mind and Body
Hannalora Leavitt & Sarah Harvey

Visit www.engagebooks.com/readers

www.ingramcontent.com/pod-product-compliance
Lightning Source LLC
Chambersburg PA
CBHW051240020426
42331CB00016B/3456